Culture Matters

MW01294204

culture matters

How to Overcome Cultural Differences in Business
Avoid the mistakes that everyone else makes when doing business internationally
By Chris Smit MSc

Completely updated, revised and expanded (v3.2 2015)
http://culturematters.com

culture matters

T 21555

culture matters

Why I wrote this book

Background

I've been working with different cultures since 1993. I have lived in three countries namely the USA, The Netherlands & Belgium. My youngest daughter is half Indian. I've had a decent exposure to different cultures and have always loved it.

The first time we went to the US was in 1976, I was 13 years old then. Going to the US in those days was rather unique and not as common as it is today. We went to Woodstock (yes, the Woodstock), 90 miles north of New York. My first cultural surprise was when my father and I went to Hertz car rental where we had reserved a car. An enormous Chevrolet of some sort. V8 engine, automatic everything. We started the engine and weren't sure if it was running because we couldn't hear a thing. Quite a difference with the Fiat 127 we had back home.

I hardly spoke a word of English when we went but learned fast. I had to. I was going to 8th-grade high school, a regular American School, with American football and all. I didn't know what was going on the first time it happened: at 8.45am the school bell rang. We were in class and everyone stood up. Right hand on their heart, back straight; The pledge of allegiance. I was clueless and thought I had ended up in the army. Why did they do this? We didn't do this at home? What's going on?

Understanding the differences in cultures has never been easy. I can remember my teacher/coach/trainer, who will remain

culture matters

anonymous, who confused me more than actually teaching me something on the field of cultural differences and diversity.

Then there are quite a number of books out there; books that are generally 500 pages or more. Most of us don't have or don't take the time to actually read those long and elaborate books. They're either too elaborate and or too detailed. Application, practical and how to's are hard to find.

The combination of the three points above: loving cultural differences, my confusing teacher/trainer/coach, the thick books already available, made me write this book.

One of my objectives is to give you a comprehensive overview of what makes sense to know, keep it practical and illustrate it here and there with a story.

Culture is a complex "*thing*" and with reading this book you should be sufficiently equipped to much better understand your world around you.

Not that you will not make any mistakes anymore or that you will not offend people from other cultures. That will be impossible. But if you can avoid one mistake, already that's an improvement of 100%!

Workshop

What you will read in this book works!

Why am I so certain about this? Well, I've been giving workshops, lectures and coaching worldwide on this topic using the structure, which is laid out in this book.

Thousands and thousands of people have benefited from one and two-day workshops, and now you can too with this book.

If you're interested in following a live workshop (1 day and 2 days) please **contact me here** (http://culturematters.com/contact-us/).

You can also invite me as a keynote speaker at your (corporate) event. Presentations can be anywhere from 40 minutes to 2 hours and are always interactive, educational and entertaining.

culture matters

Table Of Contents

Table of Contents

culture matters

culture matters

What this book can do for You, and How to Use it

This book was and is initially intended to be an eBook. But some people do prefer a paper version, so I have created a *"hybrid"* version. One that works on an eReader and that works on paper as well.

In the eBook version, there are links to several YouTube video's. When you're connected to the internet, you can watch those video's that will explain certain aspects of culture even in more detail.

Obviously in this paper version that doesn't work.

Throughout this book you will see the following image:

When you're reading this on an eReader, you can simply click the image and you'll be taken to the YouTube video.

If you're reading this on paper, you see a so called URL or Web address underneath the YouTube image.

You can type this URL in your browser (tablet, smartphone or computer) and you'll still be able to see the video.

In addition, throughout this book there are several other links that, in the eBook, will bring you to other resources supporting this book.

These are simply added with the appropriate web address.

Should you find any links that don't work, I would really appreciate if you could let me know. I will gladly send you a corrected version for free.

Should you know of other resources that would be appropriate here, you can also let me know, and I can add them to later versions.

A big thank you.

culture matters

Some Notes in the Margin

This book is not meant to be complete. I wonder if a 500-page book can be complete when it comes to cultural differences. But this book will equip you to know the necessities for you to better understand the world around you, and your own world.

My estimation is that you will finish this book in about 2 hours. After that, you can always refer to it later when necessary.

On the accompanying website Culture Matters, (http://culturematters.com) you will find a list of countries and how they score on 4 dimensions of culture. This list is handy to consult when you find yourself in a new or different culture. Click here (http://culturematters.com/how-to-use-the-cultural-reference-sheet/) for an explanation on how to use this Cultural Reference Sheet.

In my workshops, I usually advise people to discuss these cultural differences together with this list to overcome any initial cultural differences. I would advise you to do the same.

A discussion about cultural differences with your counterpart together with this list will make any cultural differences much easier to discuss and less emotionally charged.

Finally, I would like to ask you **not** to make illegal copies of this book. Rather send people who are interested in the website. A lot of work has gone into this book. I'm sure you understand my point.

culture matters

Thanks for your interest in this book. Enjoy the reading and the videos!

culture matters

Why being Culturally Competent is essential to succeed in business these days?

Globalization

Is the world becoming one?

There are some good signs of thinking so. Here are a couple:

The Internet; everyone is online and connected.

McDonalds; it's not really about McDonalds here, but a Big Mac is something you can get almost everywhere. But there is an exception... read on!

The Dollar or Euro; currencies are converging more and more. Paying with the Euro in the Euro zone has made the inter-European trade a lot easier.

English; more and more people speak English, closing the language gap that has separated cultures for so long.

There are probably more arguments that will support that the world will become one within say 50 years time and that different cultures will be a thing of the past then.

But I disagree.

Consider the following list, and see with which one's you agree or disagree.

1. The world is essentially a global village

2. One could live in any country in the world if one were honest and well intentioned

3. Business is business in any country

culture matters

4. National cultures will be a thing of the past fifty years from now and beyond

With how many do you agree? I disagree with all of them. Here are my arguments:

1. Let's look at McDonalds again. You would think a Big Mac is a Big Mac right? In fact, it is, but it's not only about the Big Mac. There is more. If I go to London and order a Big Mac, I get a Big Mac. And what if I would want a beer with my Big Mac? Ah, for that you need to go to Brussels or Paris. There you can get a beer with everything they serve[1]. And how about New Delhi India? There they don't serve beef burgers at McDonalds.

2. Here the word "*Honest*" is the tricky word. What is being perceived as being honest in one country is seen as bribery in another country.

***

---

[1] You do need to order a food item though. Even an ice cream will do; you can't only buy a beer at McDonalds in France or Belgium.

During a workshop I did for Nike some time back, I was discussing this point of honesty with someone from Turkey. He very much agreed with my standpoint that honesty is not the same in every culture. Nike, being an American company, has a lot of its sports apparel made in Turkey. In addition, Nike works with a so called "*no gift policy.*" Meaning that you were not allowed to give or receive gifts when doing business. The man from Turkey told me that that didn't work in his country. He said that he had to give "*gifts*" here and there to so-called "*grease the wheels,*" otherwise things wouldn't work at all.

***

3. When you look at giving (business) gifts, the world is not one. In some countries that is seen as dishonest, in other countries it is just the way to do business. See also me previous argument.

4. I also disagree with the last one. All over the world culture and countries are struggling to understand each other. Will the UK remain in the EU? Will the Euro hold up? What will happen in the Middle East?

The important thing to realize here is that all the things that most of us would consider as being part of the so-called Globalization,

actually don't go that deep into a culture, but rather remain on a more superficial level.

Consider the following illustration:

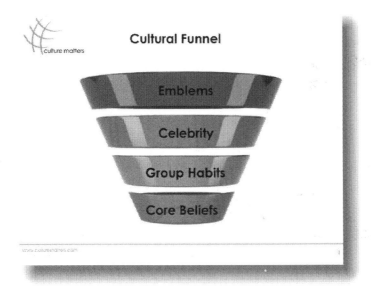

What a lot of people call Globalization happens on the top level of this funnel. The level of Emblems or symbols. Think about it:

The fact that there are a lot of people online on the Internet doesn't mean they do the same things online. Besides, the majority of the world population still isn't online. In addition in certain countries websites like Facebook and YouTube are not allowed.

culture matters

***

One day I received an email from someone in China. In his email, he said that he wanted to buy this book, but couldn't because in China he didn't have access to Amazon.com. I replied back to him saying he could send me a self-addressed and I'll send you the book. At first I thought he was joking, but a few weeks later his self-addressed envelope arrived per mail. Of course, I promptly send him the book.

***

What we eat, for instance, McDonalds food, does not answer a number of other questions that have to do with eating and food. Consider the following: We all eat, but why we eat, when we eat, why we eat, and how we eat are not culturally neutral.

A currency denomination only scratches the surface. It really doesn't go that deep. The introduction of the Euro in a number of European countries has not brought those cultures any closer together. It has become easier to cross borders in Europe, but the French aren't any less French, neither are the Germans less German etc.

The fact that the UK still does not want to join the Euro zone, has much more to do with their reluctance against being tied down by Brussels with all sorts of rules and restrictions than it has economic reasons.

Language is a symbolic way of communicating with each other. It says nothing about how you say what you say and the actual meaning you would like to get across. In other words, language is much more than words alone.

All the above-mentioned examples are on the outside of culture and diversity. They don't go that deep and can relatively be changed easily.

If you're wearing a three-piece suit and you arrive at a scene where the dress code is a lot less formal, you can easily take off your jacket and roll up your sleeves and you quickly look a lot less formal. Dress code as such, is also a symbolic expression of culture.

culture matters

What is Being Culturally Competent?

According to Wikipedia the words "*Culturally Competent*" mean: "**Cultural competence** *refers to an ability to interact effectively with people of different cultures and socio-economic backgrounds*"[2].

But this chapter deserves a bit more words. For me being Culturally Competent means that you are able to assess the situation you are in from a cultural perspective, weigh the social importance of the actors involved, including yourself, and then being able to interact with each other respectfully and constructively.

That doesn't mean that in every situation that you will find yourself in you will do the "*right thing*". You will certainly keep making mistakes, as you would in a situation where culture does not play a role.

What's important to realize is that cultural competence is a skill that can be learned.

It Takes Time

Becoming culturally competent takes time. Usually a lot of time. Let me use the analogy of walking to explain the effort it takes to become culturally competent.

The process of walking is an extremely difficult balancing act of the body and the brain. It is a constant falling forward, and

---

[2] This is only part of Wikipedia's definition. For the complete Wikipedia article click here. (http://en.wikipedia.org/wiki/Cultural_competence)

stopping that same falling forward to repeat the process with the other leg again. Ultimately this is called walking.

When we're born we cannot walk. And if you observe young children learning or trying to walk, you see their struggle of falling and getting up and starting over again.

The same holds true for becoming culturally competent. It is a constant effort of falling, getting up, and starting over again, this time being a bit more experienced.

Learning how to walk takes us about a year. I would guestimate the same for becoming culturally competent. Assuming you work in an international and/or culturally diverse situation and interact with people from different cultures on a frequent basis.

The following video illustrates the importance of Cultural Competence.

http://culturematters.com/CulturalCompetence

culture matters

Should I Adapt, or Should They Adapt?

I get this question every single workshop I give. And the answer usually is "*It depends*". Let me explain.

In an ideal world all cultures involved, when working internationally, should be culturally competent, or at least be aware of the cultural differences, what they are and why they are what they are. In other words, everyone should be culturally aware and understand the other culture.

But... this is hardly ever the case. So what do you do when you are culturally aware and even culturally competent, but *"the other one"* isn't? Here comes my answer again: It depends.

If you want something from that other person who is from a different culture, it probably makes the most sense that you adapt to the other culture. Because if you don't, the chances are that you don't get what you want. And we all know that changing or adapting yourself is by far easier than to change someone else.

If the other party wants something from you, there might be some more room to expect that the other comes a bit more your way and adapts to you.

And then there is always human dignity where it doesn't hurt to accommodate the other culture if you know you should and if you know how as well.

Often, however, we're not aware of the differences in culture and often we don't know if or when we have done something wrong towards the other culture.

culture matters

It takes a great deal of cultural awareness and understanding to know what to adapt to and what to do (and not do) to avoid uncomfortable situations and cultural clashes.

Since those friction points are often not made explicit in a conversation or other kinds of interaction, they remain under the surface, but definitely will influence perceptions.

It's like going to a restaurant for dinner and not telling the waiter the food wasn't actually that good, but never returning to that restaurant again, because it has left the impression and perception of being a lousy restaurant.

My advice is to talk about these differences, to make them more explicit. That is of course if you're able to spot them.

culture matters

A Model of Culture

There are many models of culture. Some are brilliant, others are... not so brilliant.

Probably the best-known model is the cultural framework that has been developed by Prof. Geert Hofstede. You can find Hofstede's site here. (http://www.geerthofstede.nl/)

In this book, I will focus only on the first four dimensions of Hofstede's model. Hofstede has developed two more dimensions (Long term orientation versus Short-term orientation (LTO) and Indulgence versus Restraint (IND). However, these last two dimensions do not seem to be very "*stable*" as we look at the scientific data. The scores on LTO have changed considerably over the past decade and the academic critique on the last dimension, IND, is quite significant.

So my focus will be on the first four dimensions only and with that I have added my own empirical experience and interpretation. In other words, the wording and descriptions are all mine and not Hofstede's literally.

The first four cultural dimensions are:

Hierarchy (HI): this dimension says something about people being dependent or not on the power holder, and the level of equality in a society. In high-scoring countries, the boss is the boss, which means there is less equality. In low-scoring countries, the boss is just that, the boss. This means that there is more power equality. Which shows in more functional differences rather than hierarchical differences.

culture matters

We versus I (WI): this dimension says something about where people's loyalty is. In high scoring countries one's loyalty is first with oneself and only second with the group. In low scoring countries it is the other way around. Low scoring countries have so called "*In Groups*", where high scoring countries think more according to the lines of Me, Myself & I.

Process versus Goals (PG): when it comes to name giving, this is a dimension that probably would be better off with another name than the original: Masculinity. Although the original name has nothing to do with gender differences, it often seems hard to convince people thereof.

In any case, this dimension says something about what society expects from an individual. In high scoring countries (Masculine, Tough, or Goal oriented) there is relatively little role overlap. Men do what men should do and women do what women should do.

In low-scoring countries (Feminine, Tender, or Process oriented) there is much more role overlap. Both men and women perform the same tasks. Both at home and at the office.

Anxiety Avoidance (AA): the most difficult dimension to understand for most of us. This dimension says something about the amount of structure and rules a culture wants and needs. High-scoring countries have more official and unofficial rules than low scoring countries.

This may sound obvious, but in a culture that scores high on this dimension, and thus should have a lot of rules and regulations, it is **not** always the case that people follow all the rules.

culture matters

So there might be lots of rules and people simply follow the rule that makes the most sense to them at that particular moment and situation. Granted, this is one of the most difficult of the four dimensions to understand.

For this reason, I have written a complete book dedicated to this single dimension. It gives a better understanding of the reach of this cultural dimension. It's available exclusively on Amazon.com

(http://culturematters.com/ua)

Obviously there is much more to each of these dimensions. If you're not too familiar with them, it makes good sense to read a bit more about them before you continue with this book.

Here are a couple of good (and free) resources to get you up to speed on Anxiety Avoidance:

- Wikipedia
  (http://en.wikipedia.org/wiki/Uncertainty_avoidance)

- What is Uncertainty Avoidance
  (http://culturematters.com/what-is-uncertainty-avoidance/)

- Examples of Uncertainty Avoidance
  (http://culturematters.com/examples-of-uncertainty-avoidance/)

- Uncertainty Avoidance, the United States and the Credit Crisis (http://culturematters.com/uncertainty-avoidance-the-united-states-and-the-credit-crisis/

culture matters

For more information on the other three dimension check out the following resource:

- Hofstede's cultural dimensions (Wikipedia) (https://en.wikipedia.org/wiki/Hofstede%27s_cultural_dimensions_theory) This covers a good deal of all six dimensions, plus some of the critique on his work.

Of course, there are more models of culture out there, but the Hofstede model was the first one and according to me the most applicable and easy to understand and use.

And I think that's the important part, to be able to use a model rather than having a model for the sake of having a model.

culture matters

Next are two video's of Professor Geert Hofstede explaining two of the previously mentioned dimensions in his own words.

Power Distance

http://culturematters.com/PowerDistance (Hierarchy)

Individualism

http://culturematters.com/Individualism (We versus I)

Next up is a video explaining Hofstede's dimensions of culture with a view of the world map and the distribution of each of the dimensions.

http://culturematters.com/WorldMap

culture matters

From Dimensions To Clusters

The four dimensions found by Hofstede offer one of the most practical, easy to understand and useful cultural models available. Having said that, memorizing every country with every score on every dimension is not for everyone.

For a simplified list of countries derived from the scores of Hofstede's dimensions click here. (http://culturematters.com/cultural-reference-sheet/)

Isn't there an easier, possibly even better way to understand different cultures?

Fortunately there is. It is called "*Culture Clusters*".

The idea of clustering specific cultures together is not new. Several authors and researchers have done this already. For some examples click here (http://usj.sagepub.com/content/41/3/507) and here. (http://www.tlu.ee/~sirvir/IKM/Leadership Dimensions/clusters_of_world_culture.html)

Clustering cultures offers the added benefit of having not to memorize all the countries with all the scores. Plus by clustering countries we lose very little value in terms of explaining what makes one culture different from the other.

The way you use these culture clusters is that you study the cluster you're dealing with when you're doing business with that specific cluster and compare it with your own cluster. The difference between your own and the other cluster will help you in your cultural competence.

culture matters

Because culture and cultural difference can sometimes touch on sensitive topics there are a couple of important notes in the margin before we continue.

This primarily to be able to make proper nuances when we're clustering cultures and hence putting different countries and cultures in one group, a cluster.

culture matters

One Culture is Not the Same as the Other

Let me give an example: It is not that hard to imagine that the United States (as a culture) fits relatively easily with the culture of the United Kingdom. Both speak English; the scores on the first four dimensions of culture of both countries are almost identical when you look at the individual numbers on Hofstede's dimensions. BUT (in capitals), it would be a mistake to equal Americans with Britons.

An American is not the same or identical as a Brit. American culture is not the exact same as the UK culture. Here's the point: the two cultures are *comparable*, but not identical.

Much like the Dutch language and the German language. They are not the same, but they're comparable. So never call an American being the same as a Briton and nor should you call a German a Dutchman and vice versa for both examples.

Resistance

In my workshops, I explain culture clusters pretty much the same way.

Still occasionally there is resistance from people to be compared with someone from a country that also fits that specific culture.

For instance, when I was in Ireland I asked a couple of Irishmen if their culture was comparable (not the same) as that of the British.

Guess what their answer was? A full NO. They all thought that the Irish culture is closer to the American culture.

While from a cultural perspective all three fit in the same culture cluster.

Again, the keyword here is comparable. Countries in clusters are not the same, but they are comparable or similar.

culture matters

The Fish in the Bowl

There is an old Arab saying: *"Fish will discover water last."*

What this means within the context of culture is that we only tend to realize that we have a culture of our own when we're taken out of our own culture.

Under normal circumstances, we don't question the things around us, but rather accept them just as they are.

This makes us a fish in our own bowl when we're in our own culture.

The **important** implication of this is, that it is generally very difficult to describe our own culture or to *"see"* our culture.

It is usually easier for someone from another culture to describe our culture than to describe his or her own culture.

We don't really know our own culture that well. We simply take it as it is, and tend to consider it normal, or the norm.

culture matters

InteR-Cultural versus IntrA-Cultural Differences

A remark I very often get during my workshops is that *"Yes, there are cultural differences between Americans and Indians, but within the USA and within India there are also cultural differences. What about those?".*

The difference within an or any country is so called intrA-cultural differences rather than inteR-cultural differences. However, despite the fact that every country in the world has those so-called intrA-cultural differences, most countries, with a few exceptions, are more homogeneous than they are heterogeneous. But yes, there are differences within a country as well.

The thing is that you have to have so much experience (i.e. having lived there for a number of years) to see those intrA-cultural differences. In other words, an Indian looking at an American will just see *"an American"*. While an American looking at another American will see those intrA-cultural differences.

The same holds true for an American looking at an Indian. He will just see an Indian and will not be able to tell which part of India the *"Indian"* is from.

Study habits...

A Word on Bureaucracy

A special word on bureaucracy.

Hofstede's fourth dimension covers this need for rules and the aspects of bureaucracy. But the word bureaucracy seems to be confusing people. When you ask anyone and I have asked many people over the years: "*Do you think your country or culture has a lot of rules*", indiscriminately people will give you a big "*Yes*".

So in other words people all over the world think that their country has a lot and often too many rules. This is a very objective viewpoint.

Objectively seen there are many levels of bureaucracy and hence in a number of rules cultures have (remember, rules can be official and unofficial). E.g. the UK does not have a written constitution and in Belgium every (official) document needs a stamp to make it more official.

The perception that people all over the world have is that their country is very bureaucratic often having too many rules for everything. However, if you start measuring things more objectively you will clearly see differences in the number of rules a culture has.

One example is "*the ease of doing business index*" which lists a number of countries and rates them according to how easy or difficult it is to do business with that country.

Currently, Singapore is the easiest country to do business with while in Eritrea it is a lot harder.

culture matters

A link to this information can be found <u>here</u>.

(http://www.doingbusiness.org/rankings)

culture matters

Changing Cultures; Comparing Apples with Apples

People often ask me: *"Aren't cultures changing?"*. The answer is yes, and it doesn't have an impact on the cultural differences.

Often their argument is that they see their own world changing around them and, of course, this is true.

Fifty years ago the US looked a lot different from how it looks now. But the same holds true for Italy, India, China and every other country in the world.

We're all changing and if we're all changing then the relative differences between cultures remain the same.

Let me give an example: if you could ask your grandparents if they had more respect for authority they would most certainly say Yes. But this is true for all grandparents from all countries.

Fifty years ago we all had more respect for authority. Now we all have somewhat less respect for authority, which makes that the differences remain the same.

It's something like: when the tide goes up, all ships rise.

And saying something about only one culture has very little meaning. We can only speak meaningfully about cultural differences by the grace of comparison.

So when we compare different cultures with each other, we need to make sure we're comparing apples with apples and not apples with oranges.

culture matters

The Culture Clusters

With the previous notes in the margin taken into account, it is time to introduce the 7 Culture Clusters.

They are:

- Relationship Cluster
- Tower Cluster
- iTask Cluster
- Clockwork Cluster
- Solar Cluster
- Seesaw Cluster
- Challenge Cluster

Lets discuss them one by one.

Relationship Cluster

This cluster is called Relationship cluster because the human interactions revolve mainly around relationships. Relationships through all layers of society.

Yes, there is a strong hierarchy, but the relationships that people form tend to be relatively informal. So it is relatively easy for a subordinate to talk to his boss. Both in formal and in informal situations.

Vice versa, it is expected from the boss to mingle with his people.

culture matters

You can see the boss as the Father Figure of the state, of the organization, of the department, of the family. The so-called good father.

This culture cluster "*covers*" an enormous amount of people, but not as many countries as the next cluster. The key "*word*" in this cluster is Relationship. The different so-called in-groups make up the groups, the society, and the country.

culture matters

Criteria

The trends in terms of high and low of Hofstede's dimensions are the following:

HI: high; there is a relatively strong hierarchy and the boss is clearly the boss.

WI: all the countries in this cluster are collectivistic. There is a relatively strong in-group-feel and people's loyalty is with their own group first and second with themselves. It's relationships over task.

PG: although there are few countries that score really high on this dimension, the countries that fit this cluster description can all still be called relatively masculine or tough, or goal-oriented, which ever you prefer.

AA: only on the dimension Anxiety avoidance does this dimension differ from the next one, the Tower cluster. Countries in this cluster all score relatively low. This means that the people have less of an intrinsic need for rules and regulations. Less than the Tower cluster.

Of course, there are rules and strangely there are quite a number of them. More so than in the Challenge cluster that also scores relatively low on this dimension. But the rules are intended to serve the power holder; the rules are there to keep the power holder in power, not because the people need or want rules.

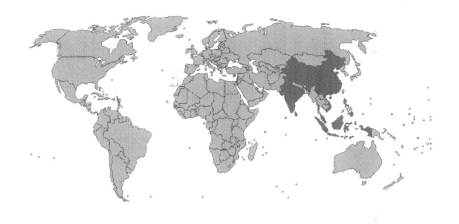

Countries

The countries in this Relationship cluster are:

- China
- India
- Vietnam
- Singapore
- Philippines
- Malaysia
- Indonesia

culture matters

Doing Business with the Relationship cluster

Follow the hierarchy.

Since the level of hierarchy is relatively high, skipping a level of management to get things done is something that you don't do.

If you do need access to someone higher up the ladder it makes more sense that someone from your side who is higher in the ranks does this. Possibly what might work is that you Cc your boss when emailing the person in (e.g.) India. This way the receiver sees that higher management is in the loop of things.

Show respect for the in-group harmony.

In other words if you're from an individualistic culture, make sure you invest in the relationship. This will take time, but it will absolutely benefit you if you do.

When you contact your counterpart in China, make it a habit to also contact him when you don't necessarily need something at that moment. I call these "*happiness calls*", or "*how are you doing calls*". Hereby you invest in the relationship you're building with that person, plus you're showing an interest.

Don't know what to talk about with your Indian colleague? Why not take a quick look at the Indian Times online, and see what's in the news at that moment. (http://www.indiatimes.com/)

Add context to your questions.

Asking your Indonesian counterpart if she can get things done in the next two weeks might not result in the desired response, but more so in a socially desirable answer. Instead, explain why you

culture matters

need what you need; how your colleague can help you; why your deadline is what it is; how you can help her, etc.

Add more context around your question rather than communicating too directly.

culture matters

A Story

I have been married to an Indian for about 10 years. I can clearly remember the first day, or actually the first moment that I was introduced to my Indian in-laws when we first met in Calcutta.

Our arrival from Amsterdam into Calcutta was late; we arrived at the apartment of my in-laws almost early morning local time. We went straight to bed. The next morning before breakfast we sat down in the living room.

And then the odd thing happened. At least for me.

What happened was actually nothing. Nothing happened, nothing was said. We simply sat there: my in-laws my wife-to-be and myself.

This situation of nothing happening and nothing being said took an enormous 45 minutes (forty-five minutes)!

It is no joke. We just sat there, doing and saying nothing.

culture matters

Explaining the Story

My cultural explanation of this situation can be found in the dimension We versus I. More We oriented cultures put more importance on the relationship. More I oriented cultures focus more on the task.

Indians are by far more We oriented than the Dutch. In other words in India relationships are a lot more important than they are in the Netherlands. I oriented cultures tend to put a lot of emphasis on the spoken word. "*Being*" for the sake of being is something that is for many Westerns a difficult concept to comprehend. Indians can easily "*be*". Just be, nothing more.

In that first meeting with my in-laws-to-be, we just were. We didn't have to do anything. Just being with each other was enough. It was a difficult lesson for me to learn, but one that I have used in many workshops.

I would start a workshop by just sitting there, and being silent (this was a series of workshops for a big Dutch bank). Every time in less than a few minutes a Dutch participant would ask me when we would eventually start the workshop.

When I would tell them we had already started, started by "*being*", it took some time for the Dutch participants to understand the point. But it had its positive effect in them understanding the difference between being relationship oriented and being task oriented.

culture matters

Tower Cluster

To a great extent does the Tower cluster resemble the previous Relationship cluster. The big difference is that relationships are equally important, but there tends to be a lot more formality. Hence the name Tower, which indicates a well-organized structure.

The Tower cluster and the Relationship cluster score very similar on three of the four dimensions of Hofstede's model of culture.

Only the fourth dimension is significantly different; countries in this cluster score relatively high. This difference justifies a separate cluster because the implications of doing business are significantly different compared with the previous cluster.

culture matters

Criteria

The trends in terms of high and low of Hofstede's dimensions are the following:

HI: high; there is a relatively strong hierarchy, and the boss is clearly the boss.

WI: all the countries in this cluster are We oriented. There is a relatively strong in-group-feel, people's loyalty is with their own group first and second with themselves.

PG: most countries in this cluster score around the middle with a few exceptions that score slightly higher than the middle.

AA: as mentioned before the countries in this cluster all score relatively high compared to the previous cluster on this dimension.

This means that there are not only many rules, but people in these countries feel there is a justified need for those rules to be there. Not only rules though, also regulations, structure and predictability are important. These rules can be official, as stated by the law, or unofficial, stemming more from habit and customs.

Although, as stated earlier, countries that score high on this dimension might not always follow the rules. Or the number of rules is so confusing, overwhelming and/or overlapping that people pick the rule that best suits them at that particular moment.

Countries

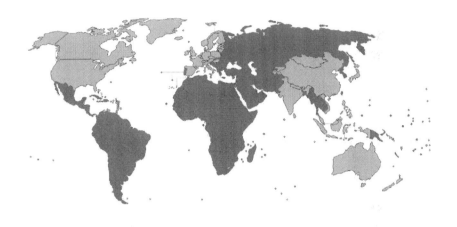

culture matters

The countries in this Tower cluster are many. Together with the Relationship cluster they cover about 80% of the world population!

- Mexico
- Middle & South America
- The whole of Africa (with the exception of the British educated in South Africa)
- Portugal
- Greece
- Turkey
- Bulgaria
- Romania
- Albania
- Russia (and former USSR countries like Ukraine)
- All other former Soviet states
- Taiwan
- Thailand
- Myanmar
- Korea (both North & South)
- Pakistan
- Sri Lanka
- Middle East

culture matters

- Most islands in the Pacific Ocean

culture matters

Doing Business With the Tower Cluster

Doing business with the Tower cluster is very comparable to doing business with the Relationship cluster. With the exception of the difference in Anxiety Avoidance.

This means that you will need to add a great level of detail to any of your plans and emails and explanations, etc.

A good amount of context theory helps in getting your point across. E.g. when you're writing a business proposal it can help by adding your understanding of your counter part's position. Or adding why you're writing this proposal or why you're using this or that solution. Don't just say it's the best solution, tell people why.

In other words, what you want to do is to eliminate the possible and perceived risk that comes with doing business with you.

Expect a fair amount of formality in doing business. Both in dress code and in the business rituals like meetings, greetings and dining out.

Next to formal formality, there will also be an informal formality. These are the unwritten rules that are not always easy to observe. My general advice is to simply go with the flow. For example when you're offered something to eat or are asked to do something accept it rather than reject it.

For other helpful tips, please read the section Doing Business With the Relationship Cluster or go over the articles mentioned earlier on Anxiety Avoidance. Because the main difference is the

cultural dimension Anxiety Avoidance it makes sense to make sure you have a good understanding of this dimension.

culture matters

A Story

Sometimes a country has so many rules that it is not easy or even impossible for an individual to know which rules apply or which procedure to follow.

A simple solution to this confusing situation is to pick the rule or process that makes the most sense to the person at that particular moment.

Take Athens, Greece as an example. This capital of Greece, as many other capitals in the world, is flooded with too many cars. Too many cars produce a lot of pollution.

In an attempt to fight pollution, the local government in Athens issued a rule stating that cars with odd numbers in their license plates were not allowed to be on the road on the even days.

So a car having the numbers "459" in it was not allowed on the road on days the 2nd, 4th, 6th, etc. of the month.

But what do you do if you need to go somewhere and your car is not allowed to be on the road because of its license plate?

Exactly, you buy two cars, one with an odd numbered license plate, and one with an even-numbered license plate. Problem solved.

culture matters

The Story Explained

I don't think this story needs a lot more explanation. What is important to realize is that even in cultures that score high on the dimension uncertainty avoidance, in other words where there are a lot of rules, people might not always follow the rules.

Only if the "*power holder*" (government, police, the boss) is there to inspect what needs to be done, people will follow the rules. If the power holder is not there to inspect what needs to be done, people might do what is best for them at that moment.

At that moment, people will pick the rule that makes the most sense and suits them best.

iTask Cluster

The name iTask comes from the individualistic nature of this cluster; everyone does his and her own thing. People leave each other alone as much as possible and are also not always aware of what the other is actually doing. But all in all, all those iTasks added together will make the organization work.

This is much like each individual representing one gear of a machine, but all gears added together will make the complete functioning machine.

The iTask cluster is a relatively small cluster when it comes to the number of countries, but economically significant, and culturally quite different form the other clusters.

Criteria

The trends in terms of high and low of Hofstede's dimensions are the following:

HI: Low. Hierarchical differences are seen as functional, rather than pure hierarchical and/or existential. In other words, the boss does something different than his subordinates. He is not better or more and likely will not have any more privileges than his subordinates.

WI: people are I oriented. Their loyalty is with themselves first and only then by the group. It is *me, myself and I thinking*".

PG: low. The only cluster where all countries score quite low on this dimension. In other words, they are feminine, process oriented, or tender countries. This separates this cluster from all other clusters[3].

AA: mostly low with some countries scoring in the middle. Most countries score low, only the Netherlands scores in the middle of this dimension.

---

[3] Make sure you understand what the word Feminine means in this context. You can go back to the explanation of Hofstede's dimension of culture earlier in this book.

Countries

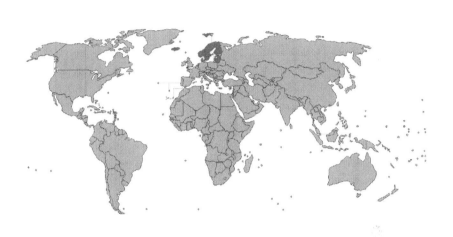

The countries that make up this cluster are:

- The Netherlands
- Denmark
- Norway
- Sweden
- Finland
- Iceland
- Latvia

culture matters

Doing Business with the iTask Cluster

Skipping a level in the hierarchy is relatively OK. And could sometimes even be expected if the continuation of certain work or project requires so.

Taking initiative without consulting your boss can be appreciated or expected depending on the situation. In general, you could say that it is better to take initiative if there is something urgent than wait for your boss to return to give you permission. Better to beg for forgiveness than to ask for permission so to speak.

The style of management is consultative, whereby a manager will actively seek the opinions of other delegates. This can be done in meetings whereby the manager will ask his subordinates what they think is the best solution or the best next steps to be taken.

Don't be surprised if a Dane will give an opinion even if it is not asked. People from the iTask cluster always have an opinion, even if they don't have an opinion.

Work inspection does not happen that often, if at all. You're pretty much left on your own. You're expected to contribute; to be your own *"gear"* in the iTask machine.

If you don't understand something, the manager expects you to go and ask him or other colleagues for an answer or solution. People will be very surprised if you keep on struggling if you don't know how to do something or don't understand what it is that needs to be done.

The purpose of business meetings is to meet, to get together and talk, to find consensus. If decisions are taken during a meeting,

culture matters

don't be surprised that they are reversed the next time there is a meeting. This is called "*growing insight*".

Changing the already taken decisions is not done to slow down the whole process, but rather to make the end result better. Besides, the process, or road to the goal, is more relatively important than the goal itself.

culture matters

A Story

As you know I am Dutch, and mother is as well. I was having dinner with my wife and my mother in a local Belgian restaurant. My wife and my mother were having a simple spaghetti and I had a salad.

Somehow during the preparation of our food something went wrong in the kitchen of the restaurant; the spaghetti was a bit over spiced.

I ate my salad, and my wife and my mother ate whatever was OK to eat from their spaghetti. When we were done, the waiter politely asked if we had enjoyed our food.

I nodded yes, my wife said yes as well. But my mother stated a brisk and firm "*NO*". Our Belgian waiter was very, very shocked, and so were we.

My wife and I quickly explained to our waiter what had happened, because he was unable to speak. But in my mother's eyes, she was only being honest; the waiter had asked if we enjoyed our food, and my mother hadn't. So should she have lied to him then? No, of course not. If someone asks you a question, you answer that question truthfully.

The Story Explained

The Dutch are known for their directness or even their bluntness.

But it is not their intention to be overly direct, or to be blunt. It is primarily their intention to be honest. And for the Dutch, being honest usually results in being very direct, even being blunt in the eyes of other cultures.

Being less direct for a Dutchmen is really difficult, so be prepared!

Clockwork Cluster

This cluster runs like clockwork. Everything works, is on-time and technically very dependable. A possible other name for this cluster could have been *"The Well Oiled Machine"*. Hence its name: it runs like clockwork.

Have you guessed a couple of countries already?

culture matters

Criteria

The trends in terms of high and low of Hofstede's dimensions are the following:

HI: Low. Hierarchical differences are seen as functional, rather than pure hierarchical. In other words, the boss only does something different than his subordinates. He is not better or more and likely will not have any more privileges than his subordinates.

If you disagree with your boss it is OK to tell him. However, just saying you disagree won't work. You have to come up with good reasons and preferably an alternative to the current situation.

WI: people are Individualistic. Their loyalty is with the individual first and only then with the group. However, the scores are not that individualistic as for instance those of the Challenge cluster.

This means that you might see a greater emphasis for instance on the family in this cluster than in other also individualistic scoring clusters.

PG: high. To the extent that working hard and doing your best will get you rewarded. Both in terms of money and social status. Achieving the goal whatever it is, is important.

AA: high. Not the highest of all countries, but high enough to make that official rules, unofficial rules, academic titles, and structure are important and are also appreciated.

Countries

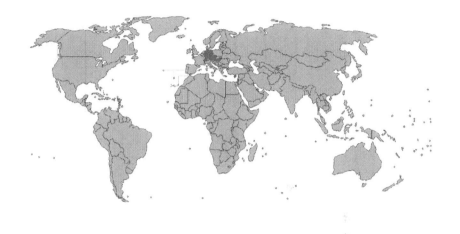

culture matters

The countries that make up this cluster are:

- Germany
- Austria
- Switzerland (German speaking part)
- Czech Republic
- Hungary
- Israel

culture matters

Doing Business with the Clockwork Cluster

Doing business with these countries is pretty straightforward. As with the iTask cluster, what you see is what you get. In general people will not have a hidden agenda.

When you're negotiating with a German or Germans, there is a good chance that you can clinch the deal then and there.

Providing you know what you're talking about, that you came prepared, and that you provided enough details. Your German counterpart will have delegated authority to make a go or no-go decision on the spot.

An on-time performance, in whatever shape or form, is important.

The Germans have a saying "*Rechtzeitigkeit ist schön fünf minuten zu spät*". Which means that if you are on time, you are actually already five minutes too late. So watch your time keeping!

Rules are important in this cluster. Official rules like keeping to the speed limit, or not crossing a zebra-crossing when the pedestrian light is red, but also unofficial rules like formal dressing, ordering a beer on tap and having to wait for 7 minutes before you actually get it ("*it needs to settle before you can drink it...*")

Because of the fact that hierarchy is low and anxiety avoidance is high, people tend to "*internalize*" the rules. This means that most people will not need a boss or someone else to check if the rules are being followed.

People tend to see the rules as *"their rules"*, and will often stick to the rules that are there.

culture matters

A Story

You might scratch your head with the following story, but it just goes to show that culture is in every aspect of society.

This story is about how clean public toilets are in three different countries and how this is culturally determined.

Depending on where you're from you might have experience with this; otherwise I hope you'll take my word for it. We're comparing three countries:

- The Netherlands
- France
- Germany; which is in this cluster being covered here

In the Netherlands going to a public toilet at a gas/petrol station on the highway is sometimes OK, but is also sometimes not OK. In other words, it depends. It depends on the attitude and mood of the person keeping the toilets clean.

When we look at the same situation in France or for that matter all the countries in the Solar cluster of which France is a part, it is highly likely that the public toilets are pretty dirty. Of course, there are exceptions, but in general, it is not a pretty picture.

Now let's go to Germany where my story comes from.

One day my wife and I were driving from the Netherlands, through Belgium to the old German town of Trier.

We parked our car in a public parking garage in the center of the city. My wife told me she had to use the restrooms/toilets. I suggested that she'd use the toilets available in the public parking

culture matters

garage. She was very hesitant. Public parking garages have a general reputation of not having the cleanest restrooms/toilets.

But she did follow my suggestion and came back with big thumbs up: the toilets were immaculately clean. Typically as you would expect from a German toilet.

culture matters

The Story Explained

Why is it that with a certain certainty you can predict the cleanliness of toilets across cultures?

In this case, it is a combination of two dimensions: Hierarchy and anxiety avoidance[4].

When Hierarchy is low and anxiety avoidance is in the middle in the case of the Netherlands, then the *"assignment"* or job of keeping the toilets clean is seen as a *"general guideline"*.

When hierarchy is high, and anxiety avoidance is high, as it is in the case of France, the *"assignment"* of keeping the toilets clean is *"externalized"*. Meaning that if the boss is not there to inspect the outcome, there is a possibility that the job doesn't get done the way it should have been. And let's face it, cleaning toilets is not the nicest job.

Now, in the case of Germany where hierarchy is low and anxiety avoidance is high, the job of toilet cleaning is *"internalized"*. Meaning that the German individual takes his job of toilet cleaning as something that is his or hers. There is no need for a boss to inspect the end result. In German one could say *"Gründlichkeit, und Pünktlichkeit muss sein"*; thoroughness and being on time are important.

---

[4] And to some extent a bit of Process versus Goals in case of the Netherlands.

Solar Cluster

The solar cluster image displays our solar system, as you can see in the image here. Where you see the boss in the middle, as being the Sun and the subordinates orbiting around him or her, as being the planets.

It is like an equilibrium; they both keep each other in balance and they both need each other; no leaders without followers and no followers without a leader.

Much like our own solar system with the planets revolving around our Sun.

culture matters

Criteria

The trends in terms of high and low of Hofstede's dimensions are the following:

HI: high. There is a clear difference between the ones in power and the ones who are not. The boss is the boss. You can see this through all layers of society.

The director of a local bank office is the boss, but when he meets his regional boss, that person is clearly the boss. And so on.

WI: high. People are individualistic. They let their own agenda prevail over that of the group and sometimes even over what their boss tells them to do.

PG: in the middle. Some countries score higher than others. But there are no real high and low scores.

AA: high. Rules, structure and predictability are important. The countries in this cluster all have a so-called *"impersonal bureaucracy"*, and often this bureaucracy is stifling business and innovation in these countries.

culture matters

Countries

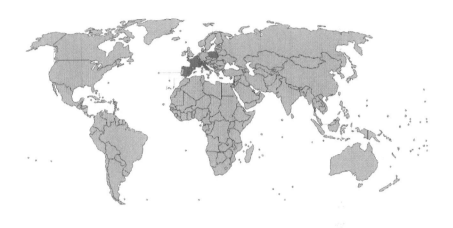

culture matters

The countries that make up this cluster are:

- Belgium (both the Dutch-speaking and the French-speaking communities)

- France

- Italy (but only the north; say from Rome and up; the south of Italy fits better in the Tower cluster)

- Spain (although they are more collectivistic than the other countries in this cluster)

- Switzerland (the French speaking community)

- Poland

culture matters

Doing Business with the Solar Cluster

Doing business in countries like France and Belgium is not as straight forward as in Germany or the Netherlands[5].

What you see is what you get, does not always apply and there might often be a second or hidden agenda's or maybe different people with their own and different agenda's.

Hierarchy is relatively high, so there will always be a boss and a boss of the boss and a boss of the boss's boss. Skipping rank is not done and not appreciated.

Countries from the Solar cluster tend to be highly conflict avoidant, which means that you might get affirmative answers to your question while the intention or final result could be quite the opposite.

When you're negotiating with the Solar cluster, you might find that the people you're directly negotiating with, will not have the ultimate decision power to carry out the deal or proposal; there is very often another boss that needs to give the final approval.

The problem is that this final decision maker was not present at your negotiations and he or she will not be familiar with the full details that were discussed during your meeting.

Therefore make sure that you provide enough context detail during your initial negotiation so that the people present at your negotiation can convey the content fully and can answer any question the decision maker might have afterward.

---

[5] This is not meant to be a negative or judgmental statement. It is merely to relatively compare countries and cultures.

The "*real*" negotiations can often take place in more informal settings like lunch and dinner occasions. Both during lunch and dinner, do not be shocked if the Frenchman will order a glass of wine. You don't have to follow, but if you want to fit in, you might just as well go with the flow.

It is by no means intended to get you drunk and then to take advantage of your intoxicated state. It is merely a way the French have their lunch. Not always, but often enough.

A Story

In a Belgian office where six people were working, the boss of the company had instructed his IT man (there was no IT department, only an IT man) to set up their email server in such a way that he, the boss, would receive a copy of EVERY email that was being sent by his staff or that was being received by his staff. Every email!

This way he would never miss a thing and he would always know what the state of affairs was of his company and what his people were up to.

The exceptional aspect with this set-up was that he had **not** told his people that he was reading each and every mail that they sent or received.

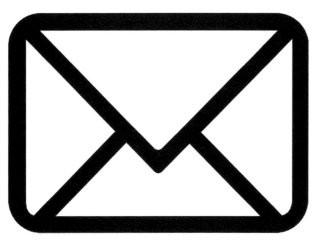

The Story Explained

The explanation of this story can be found in a combination of two dimensions: hierarchy and anxiety avoidance.

Hierarchy: he is the boss. The boss can decide to instruct the IT man to configure the email server so that he will receive all emails being sent and received.

Being the boss, he does not necessarily need to let his people know. He's the boss, he decides.

Anxiety avoidance: the urge or need to know what is going on, each and every moment with each and everyone, is an expression of this dimension.

By reading each and every email, he increases his knowledge of what is going on and thereby reduces uncertainty and increases predictability.

Seesaw Cluster

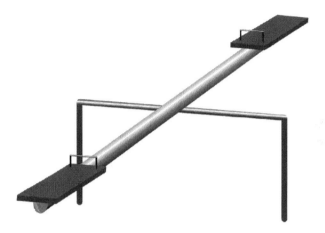

This cluster got its name because people in this society tend to keep a tight balance with everything they do in life. It is like they are standing in the middle of the seesaw and are sometimes leaning one way and sometimes leaning the other way. They're keeping a balance.

The Seesaw cluster is actually made up of only one country. But because of the economic importance of this country I've decided to make it a separate cluster.

culture matters

Criteria

There is really only one country that has this very distinct cultural profile.

HI: in the middle. Although the perception is that it should be much higher, the score is actually somewhere in the middle. Under certain circumstances, it is OK to object to what your boss tells you.

WI: in the middle. For people with a Western or Individualistic background or culture, it might seem as if this culture is much more collectivistic. But if the score difference is more than 10 points it makes no difference if it is 10, 20, or 30, it still comes across as being collectivistic in the case of Japan.

Group work works in this cluster, and still there is room for the individual as well.

PG: high. Actually very high. This country scores the highest in the cultural model of Hofstede. This makes this nation very competitive. But due to the middle score on We versus I, it might not always be visible to other, more Individualistic, Western countries. But amongst themselves every individual knows who is the best and every individual strives to be the best at what they do.

AA: high. Rules, structure and predictability are very important. Pretty much everything has to happen according to pre-set rules. Many things are ritualized to the extent that they have a beginning, a middle and an end.

Countries

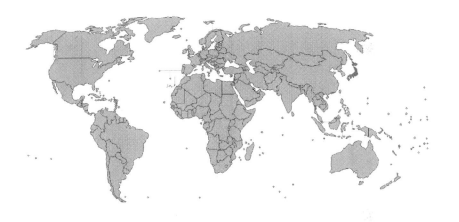

As said before, the only country in this cluster is:

- Japan

culture matters

Doing Business with the Seesaw Cluster

For most Westerns, doing business with the Japanese is the most difficult culture to do business with. This is not a value judgment about the Japanese. It is just that: for most Westerns doing business with the Japanese is very difficult.

A lot and I mean a real lot of detail is required when making proposals or writing project plans. The reason for this is the high score on AA, but also the high score on PG plays a role: Japanese want to get it right, and they do not want to loose, which potentially implies losing face.

Several rituals are very important at work. Depending on the organization you might see that at the beginning of the work day people perform a certain loyalty ritual to the boss or to the organization.

The ritual of Karaoke is meant for everyone to blow off steam and tell each other the real truth about what they think of each other or the boss or the organization, often with the help of a little alcohol.

As soon as the party is over, everyone slips back into his or her usual pattern of structure and sticks to what must be done and the rules to follow.

If ever you're invited to a Karaoke party you must go. I say and mean must, because if you don't you will often have offended your host and your business is potentially over.

When Japanese ask you for more detail about whatever you're proposing, give them more detail. But even if you think you have

culture matters

given all the possible details, there is a good chance that you will be asked to provide even more details.

Japanese are hard workers. As many other cultures are by the way. But in Japan people actually die from working too hard. This phenomenon is called "*Karōshi*" which literally means "*death from overwork*" and is an official statistic in Japan as a cause of death.

Hard work is a virtue in Japan and Japanese expect the same from you. So expect to make long hours.

In a country as organized as Japan, it is hard to imagine any conflicts. But of course, Japanese also have conflicts. But the Japanese are extremely conflict avoidant. Anything that could cause even the mildest form of upset from the standard harmony is avoided. So be very careful with giving your open hearted feedback or advice.

culture matters

A Story

The following is not really a story, but more of an example or even a bit of a joke[6].

> **This says a lot about the quality of Japanese products and their quality standards:**
>
> Apparently a Dutch international company decided to have some parts manufactured in Japan as a trial project. In the specifications, they set out that they will _only_ accept three defective parts per 10.000
>
> When the delivery came in, there was an accompanying letter:
>
> *"We, Japanese people, had a hard time understanding Dutch business practices. But the three defective parts per 10.000 have been separately manufactured and have been included in the consignment.*
>
> *Hope this pleases you !"*

---

[6] If you would interpret this as a joke, it is by no means meant to offend anyone.

culture matters

The Story Explained

I showed this story in the form of a PowerPoint slide once to a split audience: one-half was Dutch, the other half was Japanese.

The Dutch thought this was funny, the Japanese wondered what the Dutch were laughing about. In their eyes, it was logical, normal, the truth. They were not offended; they just didn't understand why the Dutch were laughing.

For the Japanese it is very important that things are done well. That everything is structured, standardized, and done to the best of their ability.

For example trains in Japan operate on time. Period.[7]

Things are manufactured according to standards and procedures. And then if you want malfunctioning stuff, you can have it, but you need to ask for it.

The two dimensions here are Process versus Goals and Anxiety avoidance.

Process versus Goals: you do the best that you can and you do that with everything. In letting trains run on time and in manufacturing, even defects. In everything.

Anxiety avoidance: doing the things like they should be done is important. This goes for running trains and for manufacturing stuff.

---

[7] In 2012 the Tokaido Shinkansen was only 0.6 minutes late; for the whole year!

Challenge Cluster

The Challenge Cluster got its name because of the fact that the countries clustered here see every possible problem not as a problem but rather as a challenge. *"We have no problems, we have only challenges"*.

Or to put it differently: the glass always tends to be half full rather than half empty.

The Challenge cluster is made up of a group of countries that are culturally closely related (although they are not identical of the same).

culture matters

Criteria

HI: low. Hierarchical differences are based on functional differences. So in general it is OK to openly disagree with your boss.

WI: high. Some countries in this cluster have the highest score on this dimension in Hofstede's model. This makes the individual focus very much on him or herself. Whereby any group activity is to the benefit of the individual, with the benefit to the group being secondary.

PG: high. Not as high as Japan, but still relatively high. Combined with the high score on Individualism makes the perception of the impact of this dimension become even stronger.

AA: low. Although there are differences within this cluster, overall people tend to be entrepreneurial, take calculated risks and are innovative.

culture matters

Countries

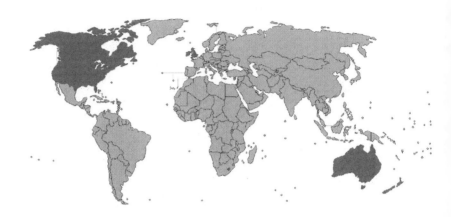

culture matters

The countries in this cluster can be combined as the so-called Anglo-Saxon countries.

- United States
- United Kingdom
- Canada
- Ireland
- Australia
- New Zealand
- The British-educated people of South Africa

culture matters

Doing Business with the Challenge Cluster

The work mentality of, typically Americans, is such that they agree to a sort of psychological contract with their employer; between 9 and 5 I work for you and I will do as I'm told. After that, we are equal again.

This could result in the perception of a strong hierarchy, which in actual fact it isn't.

Competition and winning are keywords in these countries. Reaching the goal is very important. How this goal is reached is of relative less importance (by hook or by crook).

In general, the people that you negotiate with will usually have the delegated authority to agree or disagree with your proposal.

Individual benefits are important. People listen most to the *"radio station WIIFM"*. Which stands for What's In It For Me. So make sure that you consider this when doing business.

Risk taking is seen as a positive thing. There are quite a number of quotes that illustrate this: *"No pain, no gain"* or *"No guts, no glory"*.

Competition is another one of those typical Anglo-Saxon phenomena. Competition is seen as good and as fair play. Basically, competition is a way to bring out the best in you and me.

With the high level of competitiveness, the details sometimes tend to fall between the cracks. Compared to countries like France and Germany, the detailed level of planning of Anglo-Saxons is relatively less.

culture matters

There is one form of detailed measurement that this cluster excels in, namely statistics.

Statistics and numbers are being collected about virtually everything. This is not done for the purpose of detail, which is linked to Anxiety avoidance. It is done for the purpose to convince the other and as a sales weapon to show that their product is better than that of the competition. Which makes this argument positively linked to Process versus Goals.

culture matters

A Story

For this story to make any sense to you, you would have to watch this video first:

http://culturematters.com/Reebok

After having shown this commercial in one of my workshops I did in Boston, USA, I asked if this ad had any comparison to real life.

"*Of course not*" the general answer was. Until one American participant argued: "*Well if I could get 46% productivity improvement like this, I would surely consider it...*"

culture matters

The Story Explained

Of course we all laughed when he made this remark. But it goes to show how competitive the US is.

This competitiveness is for a great part the relative high score on Process versus Goals in Anglo-Saxon countries.

But to fully understand this competitiveness you need to take the other three dimensions into account as well.

Low HI: there is no boss that will hold you back or that will tell you off.

High WI: a strong focus on the individual; *"If it's going to be, it's up to me"* is a well-known quote.

Low AA: the willingness to take risks.

culture matters

Conclusion(s)

It's not easy to draw conclusions, any conclusion when it comes to cultural differences. So I'll stick to a couple of bullet points.

- Nothing about culture is good or bad. It just is. If it was bad, people would have changed it.

- One can only talk meaningfully about a culture by the grace of comparison. So an absolute statement about any culture is nonsense.

- Culture is first experienced in the *"gut"*. Emotionally. We feel what we feel and only then we interpret this rationally and give meaning to it using our own frame of reference.

- When we are under stress and working with other cultures, we tend to go back to our *"default"* behavior, which usually makes the cultural differences more apparent and the friction between the Cultures bigger.

- We tend to blame the *"other"* Culture for what is going wrong in our eyes.

Finally ending with a quote from Carl Jung:

"Everything that irritates us about others can lead to a better understanding or ourselves."

Who is Chris Smit and How to Get in Touch?

Chris Smit is an Author, Entrepreneur, International Public Speaker, Consultant, and Interculturalist.

He has worked with thousands of individuals from over 100 nationalities in more than 45 different countries sharing his know-how on Cultural Differences and more.

My Story

My first job was with KLM Royal Dutch Airlines as an administrative intern. In total, I had 3 jobs there. The last one being the most fun and most interesting: I was a Marketing &

culture matters

Sales Consultant for the Airline. Traveling to pretty much every corner of the world helping KLM colleagues achieve their targets.

In the meantime, I went back to school. I studied and got my Master's degree in Organizational Psychology from the University of Amsterdam in 6 years doing evening school. I enjoyed every minute of it.

The combination of study and travel didn't bother me. I was working with different cultures and expanding my knowledge on what makes people tick in organizations.

In 1999, after 12 years with KLM, I decided it was time for a change. That change was a good choice because the company I started working for had a group of people all working on Intercultural Management.

I had done my University thesis using the work of Professor Geert Hofstede and now was able to work with it too. Awesome!

In 2007, I started the company Culture Matters. I wanted to fully focus on cultural differences and diversity and have been doing so ever since.

With the Internet all around us and the ongoing globalization I think it is of absolute importance to be Culturally Competent when you're working Internationally.

Fortunately, these skills can be learned. The good thing is that with proper cultural awareness education everybody *"gets it"*. I find that a promising thought.

I am passionate about giving lectures and workshops and am sure I will be for years!

culture matters

culture matters

What Other Say About Chris

Paul Wait, CEO GTMC; London, UK

"Chris is an experienced culture expert. I've been doing business with him for years and have never been disappointed.

He not only knows what he's talking about, he can also deliver it in a way that captures an audience, be it 10 people or 150 people. If culture is important to you (and for whom isn't it) work with Chris."

Christophe Scholer; CEO Araxxe, Lyon France

"We've been growing rapidly internationally, so we needed to become culturally competent. For that, we have found the perfect partner in Chris Smit. I've attended a workshop where Chris explained and taught us all we needed to know to more effectively work with our international clients.

If you're working internationally, work with Chris. He can save you time and money by letting you do your business better."

Jens Schuster; Senior Director Lufthansa City Center, Frankfurt Germany

"As a Senior Director for Lufthansa City Center International (LCCI) I deal with different cultures every day. I met Chris at a conference in Abu Dhabi, where he gave a keynote lecture. Immediately after I contracted him for our organization's annual customer event.

Chris is able to capture the attention from the very first moment on, and hold it till the last minute. He broadens and deepens your understanding, as well as giving you the tools to overcome cultural differences within a global business world."

culture matters

Hans Odenthal, People Manager Sioux Embedded Systems; Eindhoven, the Netherlands

"Chris is an open-minded flexible professional who can deliver high-quality work when it comes to culture. After having attended a workshop of him, people are better equipped to work with other cultures.

What counts for me are the end results, and for that you can count on Chris. Working with Culture Matters has increased our productivity when it comes to working with other cultures."

Brigit Law; Senior Trade Officer Dutch Embassy, Brussels Belgium

"Chris Smit offers excellent guidance in understanding the effect of cultural differences in doing business abroad. Even if, or especially when, it concerns trading with neighboring countries.

That's why I asked Chris to sit in a panel discussion about cultural differences that was linked to a business matchmaking of young entrepreneurs from The Netherlands and Belgium. Bringing these young people at an early stage in their internationalization process in contact with experts like Chris, will help them succeed in their business."

culture matters

You can reach me here:

Email: chris.smit@culturematters.com

Twitter: @chrissmit

LinkedIn: be.linkedin.com/in/smitchris

culture matters

Photo Credits

- eurekabharali10
  (http://pixabay.com/en/users/eurekabharali10)

- Wikipedia

- geralt (http://pixabay.com/en/users/geralt/)

- nice-cool-pics.com (http://nice-cool-pics.com/postcard.img31466.htm)

- Deluge (https://openclipart.org/user-detail/Deluge)

culture matters

Resource List

Below is a list of other references and books that you might find useful.

Cultural Reference Sheet

Get an overview of countries and their respective scores on 4 Culture Dimensions. Click here to get it. (http://culturematters.com/cultural-reference-sheet/)

Books

- Chris Smit, Uncertainty Avoidance in International Business: *The Hidden Cultural Dimension You Need to Understand When Doing Business Overseas*

- Björn Bjerke, Business Leadership and Culture: National Management Styles in the Global Economy
- Craig Storti, The art of crossing cultures
- Culture Shock! A guide to customs and etiquette series of books on more than 60 different countries, Times Media Private Ltd
- Edward T. Hall, The Silent Language
- Edward T. Hall, Beyond Culture
- Geert Hofstede, Culture's Consequences
- Geert Hofstede, Cultures and Organizations, Software of the Mind
- Geert Hofstede, Masculinity and Femininity

- Hofstede, Pedersen & Hofstede, <u>Exploring culture</u>
- Marieke de Mooij, <u>Global Marketing and Advertising</u>
- Marieke de Mooij, <u>Consumer Behaviour and Culture</u>
- Susan Schneider & Jean-Louis Barsoux, <u>Managing across cultures</u>
- Samuel P. Huntington <u>The Clash of Civilizations and the Remaking of World Order</u>
- Fons Trompenaars <u>Riding the Waves of Culture: Understanding Diversity in Global Business</u>

Examples of books on specific countries or regions

- Yale Richmond & Phyllis Gestrin, <u>Into Africa</u>
- Eduardo Archetti, <u>Masculinities</u>
- Jianguang Wang, <u>Westerners Through Chinese Eyes</u>
- Tony Fang, <u>Chinese Business Negotiating Style</u>
- Verner Worm, <u>Vikings And Mandarins</u>
- H. Wenzhong, & C. Grove, <u>Encountering The Chinese</u>
- Philippe d'Iribarne, <u>La Logique de l'Honneur</u> (on France, the USA and the Netherlands)
- Greg Nees, <u>Germany: Unravelling an Enigma</u>
- David Matsumoto, <u>The New Japan</u>
- Jacob Vossestein, <u>Dealing with the Dutch</u>
- Eva Kras, <u>Management in two cultures</u>
- Orlando Figes, <u>Natasha's Dance</u> (on Russia)

culture matters

- Edward Stuart & Milton Bennet, <u>American Cultural Patterns</u>
- Frank E. Hugget , <u>The Dutch Today</u>
- E.M. Goldratt, Jeff Cox, <u>The Goal</u>

Other Books

<u>200% of Nothing; a book on Statistics and Numbers</u>

culture matters

Thank you!

You've made it to the end of this book and I want to thank you for it. If you want to be kept updated on issues where <u>Culture Matters</u>, I do a Podcast where I interview real people with real experiences, who share their stories and tips on becoming more culturally competent. You can subscribe to the Podcast **here**. (https://itunes.apple.com/be/podcast/culture-matters-podcast-on/id599525836).

If you want to see a list of people that have been interviewed, you can go **here**. (http://culturematters.com/podcast-2/)

I also keep a blog on my website where I write on current affairs and put them in an Intercultural context.

In addition, you can sign up for the newsletter, which comes out 11x per year and consists of all the blog posts of the last month, and the podcast interviews.

Should you have a subject that you'd like me to write about, please <u>send me an email</u>. (http://culturematters.com/contact-us/) Also, if you'd like to write it yourself, drop me a line.

I've spent a lot of time putting this book together, so I'd like to ask you not to copy or distribute this book without my permission.

If you have any suggestions for improvement of this book they are more than welcome.

Thanks!

culture matters

Disclaimer

The information contained in this guide is for informational purposes only.

Any advice that I give is my opinion based on my own experience. You should always seek the advice of a professional before acting on something that I have published or recommended.

Please understand that there are some links contained in this guide that I may benefit from financially.

This book is partially inspired by the work of professor Geert Hofstede and his cultural models. I have primarily based the contents of this book on my own viewpoints and experience.

No part of this publication shall be reproduced, transmitted, or sold in whole or in part in any form, without the prior written consent of the author. All trademarks and registered trademarks appearing in this guide are the property of their respective owners.

Users of this guide are advised to do their own due diligence when it comes to making business decisions and all information, products, services that have been provided should be independently verified by your own qualified professionals. By reading this guide, you agree that my company and myself are not responsible for the success or failure of your business decisions relating to any information presented in this guide.

All images and photos used in this book fall under the CC Attribution License. In the case you think there is an image that

culture matters

does not fall under this license, please inform me as soon as possible. I will take corrective measures.

I have done my utmost to verify all links and videos. However should you find one link or video not working properly, please let me know by sending me an email: chris.smit@culturematters.com.

Made in the USA
San Bernardino, CA
07 April 2017